HEAL THYSELF

AN INNER GUIDE TO UNLEASHING THE POWER OF THE MIND-BODY CONNECTION FOR OPTIMAL HEALING

Arie Borealis

Pharos Books

Disclaimer Notice:

Please note the information contained within this document is for educational and entertainment purposes only. All effort has been executed to present accurate, up to date, reliable, complete information. No warranties of any kind are declared or implied. Readers acknowledge that the author is not engaged in the rendering of legal, financial, medical or professional advice. The content within this book has been derived from various sources. Please consult a licensed professional before attempting any techniques outlined in this book.

By reading this document, the reader agrees that under no circumstances is the author responsible for any losses, direct or indirect, that are incurred as a result of the use of the information contained within this document, including, but not limited to, errors, omissions, or inaccuracies.

ISBN: 978-93-59835-48-8
eISBN: 978-93-59835-92-1

Publisher: Pharos Books (P) Ltd.
Plot No.-55, Main Mother Dairy Road
Pandav Nagar, East Delhi-110092
Phone: 011-40395855, +4049916623
WhatsApp: +91 8368220032
E-mail: sales@pharosbooks.in
Website: www.pharosbooks.in
First Edition: 2024

HEAL THYSELF
By Arie Borealis

CONTENTS

INTRODUCTION

The mind-body connection is the relationship between a person's thoughts, attitudes, and actions, as well as their physical health. Although researchers have known for a long time that our feelings and thoughts can have an effect on our bodies, we are only just beginning to grasp how they influence our health and well-being.

Your mind can control your body to a much greater extent than you think. You can understand this connection and use it effectively to improve your mental and physical health and well-being. We begin with some basic questions:

- What is the nature of the body-mind connection?
- What are the mechanisms underlying this connection?
- How can I harness the power of the body-mind connection?

In chapter one, we will introduce fundamental concepts about the mind, particularly the role of attention and the 8 importance of directing one's attention to the here and now. Attention is the key to unleashing the mind's power.

Like a flashlight in a dark room, your mind deploys its resources to where your attention is focused.

Wherever your attention is focused, additional information becomes available, exactly like a flashlight in a dark room. You can direct the light beam as you choose, and wherever it is pointed, information is clearer and richer. You can have a very tight focus or a broad focus.

This is the mind's system for directing attention.

The human mind's ability to mentally travel through time is exceptional. You may easily travel to the past and future, but frequently, this ability might cause problems for your attention system. In effect, your attention is hijacked, and less time is available for the mind to experience what is happening in the present as a result.

Chapters two and three set the stage for discussions in the remaining parts of the book. In these chapters, we will learn that the mind has the power to heal the body. We discuss scientific evidence that mental beliefs can 9 influence and control bodily processes, urge you to push your boundaries, and fully use this inherent capability.

Chapters four through six will discuss the practical ways to harness the power of the mind over the body.

Techniques of visualization, self-affirmation, and positive thinking are discussed. Self-affirmative statements, if worded clearly and repeated frequently, can do wonders in helping you achieve your wellness goals.

In chapter seven, we will address one of the most important ways mind power can be used to restore and maintain health in your body, namely mind techniques for stress control. Practical methods to control and curb stress are introduced, including meditation.

The book ends with an optimistic note in chapter eight, where the amazing power of the mind and the brain to recover from trauma and adapt to changing conditions will be discussed.

Hopefully, at the end of this book, you will have a better handle on the management of your own personal universe.

CHAPTER 1

Mind and Attention

Attention is the key to unleashing the mind's power. As mentioned, it is like a flashlight in a dark room. And just like turning on a flashlight in a dark environment, directing our attention somewhere causes additional information to become accessible in that location. Your mind deploys its resources to where your attention is focused.

Attention Is the Key to Your Mind

Consider the analogy of attention being a flashlight as one way to think about it. We are able to have a laser-like focus, very tight focus, or broad focus; yet, no matter which way the flashlight is pointed, the information becomes clearer and more abundant. More details come into view, and you are able to direct it as you wish. This is the attentionalorienting and focusing system of the brain.

Attention can be diverted to any point in time. The human mind has the extraordinary capability of engaging in what is known as "mental time travel." Our ability to effortlessly travel through time, both to the past and future, can, however, frequently place our attention system in a precarious position. When this takes place, there are fewer opportunities for the mind to experience what is taking place in the present time.

We can think of going back in time not only as a method to reflect on what has occurred, but particularly when we are under a great deal of pressure and anxiety. We may find ourselves pondering, reliving, or regretting events that have already transpired in the past. Or, we jump ahead in time in a way that is counterproductive, maybe overreacting or becoming anxious about things that not only haven't taken place yet and, to be honest, may never take place at all.

The Neuroscientific Study of Attention

Studies in the field of cognitive neuroscience and brain imaging have shown that there are separate brain regions and networks that are associated with different characteristics of the human mind, specifically attention and mind wandering. The ability to focus attention–the flashlight–involves the central executive network, which includes portions of the frontal and parietal lobes of the brain, while the default mode network of the brain, also known as the "mind wandering" network, is active when a person's mind tends to wander.

These networks do not share any anatomical characteristics with one another. To put it in simpler terms, the central executive network and default mode network are dependent on distinct parts of the brain.

They inhibit one another. Thus, when the activity of one network is high, the activity levels of the other two networks are lower. This is because they are mutually inhibitory. They provide us with a clue as to the regions of the brain that may be involved in brain training requiring attention.

The Art and Science of Mind Training

The changes that take place in the brain can be analyzed from a variety of perspectives. When we want to look at structural changes in the brain, we might look at brain gyrification, which refers to how tightly packed and condensed the brain is. The brain can become smoother, or less gyrified, as we age as a result of the effects of stress or as a consequence of brain-related illnesses. A brain with more gyrification and more densepacking is a healthier brain than one with less gyrification and less dense-packing.

Research has indicated that people who engage in attention-focusing practice and mindfulness for longer periods of time have better gyrification, or the appearance of a brain that is more efficient (Luders et al., 2012). These individuals have cortical gyrification in networks that are connected to the attention system of the brain. This is a really fascinating finding because it suggests not only do certain regions of the brains of attention practitioners look healthier, but also that those are the same regions that are related to attention and control over mind wandering.

Long-term practitioners of attention and mindfulness also exhibit functional changes in their brains as a result of their practice. According to the findings of one study, individuals who have practiced focusing their attention for an extended period of time had lower levels of activity in a brain network that is associated with mind wandering (Mrazek et al., 2013). It was discovered that two important regions of the default mode network, namely the medial prefrontal cortex and posterior simulate cortex of the brain, exhibited decreased activity in attention practitioners in comparison to control subjects who were the same age and had the same level of education.

These findings suggest that not only are there structural changes, but also that the functional brain activity profiles appear to be matched with improved performance. The practitioners of attention and mindfulness appear to have improved their ability to exert authority over the operations of the mind-wandering network. However, more studies are needed so that we can get a more certain answer about whether 15 or not attention training can make the brain healthier and work more effectively than it did before.

It is really exciting that practicing attention can result in beneficial changes to the structure as well as the functioning of the brain, but there has to be more research done on the topic.

Attention and Changes in Brain Performance

Is it true that the networks in the brain that are responsible for attention become stronger and healthier with attention training? Is it true that those who participate in attention training have improved performance when completing tasks that need attention?

Unfortunately, research shows that people's attention does not remain consistent, even during times of extreme stress. If we index attention using straightforward computerbased behavioral tasks, we see that attentional performance falls after repeated weeks of high demand and stress.

Many of the investigations carried out on the cognitive effects of attention training look at groups of individuals 16 who have been put through some kind of taxing event.

For these people, paying attention can often be the difference between success and failure (such as in the case of students) or between life and death (as in the case of firemen or members of the armed forces).

Studies in these kinds of groups encourage cognitive resilience, which can be defined as the capacity to preserve or restore one's cognitive powers. In particular, the goal is to strengthen cognitive abilities such as attention and working memory, both of which are susceptible to decline. We want to ensure that they continue to function well and are safeguarded against any possible deterioration.

Training in attention has been shown to reliably improve a variety of elements of cognitive functioning, including selective attention, working memory, and mind wandering (Liu et al., 2023). When viewed through the lens of attention training as a form of brain exercise, this looks like a very encouraging finding. Training oneself to be mindful may, in the broadest sense of the phrase, be an effective technique for training one's brain.

CHAPTER 2

Mind Over Body

Your mind can control your body to a much greater extent than you think. Our minds and bodies are tied to one another. It is up to each of us to become conscious of the links between our bodies and minds, as well as cultivate a mind-body connection that is loving and harmonious.

The Extent of Mind Control Over Body

Your mind and body are responsible for your health, and while you may not have complete control over them, you do have some say in how you think and respond to the things going on around you. Let's discover some fascinating information regarding the mind-body connection:

The Mind-Body Connection Is Present in All of Us

The mind-body connection is not something that is far away or can only be obtained by devoting a significant 19 amount of time to yoga and meditation; rather, it is something that is always there. The link is something that each and every one of us is exposed to on a daily basis, regardless of whether or not we are consciously aware of it.

Natural mind-body connections are something that almost all of us have experienced at some point in our lives. Some instances of these connections are the sensation of "butterflies" in the stomach before giving a presentation or running a race, salivation in response to the sight of an appetizing-looking dish, and so on. The mind-body link can, on occasion, lead to unfavorable results, such as the inability to achieve one's academic, athletic, or professional goals due to the presence of dread brought on by the mind.

The Way We Think Influences How Our Bodies Respond

If we consistently engage in damaging, self-defeating thought patterns, our physical bodies will reflect those patterns. The physical manifestations of an emotional and mental imbalance, such as stress-induced 20 headaches, stiff shoulders, and back pain, can be the precursors of more serious health problems, such as unhealthy weight gain or loss, insomnia, and high blood pressure.

On the other hand, we have the ability to train ourselves to think more positively and cultivate good coping strategies in order to deal with the pressures and difficulties of everyday life. The state of our emotional and mental health can, over time, either be harmful or beneficial to the immune system of the body.

Our coping strategies and the ways in which we manage to deal with stress have a direct correlation with how well we deal with serious illnesses like cancer. A negative impact that chronic stress has on the body is that it can, over an extended period of time, render us more prone to developing health conditions, such as diabetes, hypertension, heart disease, and even some infections.

However, we may keep our stress levels lower, make productive use of the natural mindbody link that we all possess, and keep both our minds and bodies in good form. To put it another way, the greater our resiliency, as 21 measured by our ability to maintain composure and experience lower levels of psychological stress, the lower our levels of physical stress will be, and the lower our risk will be of getting a disease.

Your Heart Can Benefit From the Practice of Meditation

The mind and body may have a real and true link, as shown by the findings of medical research. The mindbody connections, more specifically the mind-heart connection, can be altered via the use of practices such as meditation and other relaxation techniques (Merschel, 2022). Although there are few studies that specifically address how mindheart therapies can aid patients with congestive heart failure, meditation might help with depression, which frequently occurs in conjunction with heart disease.

Anyone who wants to maintain their sense of composure throughout the day can benefit from meditating for roughly 15 minutes each day. Mental impressions and reactions to circumstances can be shifted through the practice of meditation and other similar activities. When 22 you become conscious of feelings of stress and anxiety and then control your breathing, both your mind and body begin to relax. Even if you only have a few seconds to spare during a hectic day, practicing calm breathing can have the same beneficial effects.

How Does Your Mind Control Your Body?

We are all aware that the brain is capable of managing and regulating a wide variety of processes throughout the rest of the body. However, to what extent can we influence and control the work that our brain is performing in its role as CEO of the body?

It's surprising to discover how powerful and far-reaching the effects of only one or two conscious or unconscious ideas may be. When an idea enters the brain, the rest follows automatically, regardless of whether we like it or not. Behind the scenes of our conscious awareness, all of the physiological responses that result from either our 23 deliberate or unconscious thought processes are playing out.

For instance, is it possible that the thoughts that are running unconsciously through our minds incessantly create a cascade of chemical reactions that form what we feel and the manner in which we feel it? Can the long-term impacts of our habitual thinking be the reason why our bodies move into a state of imbalance, which we refer to as disease? Is it possible that the thoughts that we have from second-to-second will eventually cause our bodies to become unhealthy? What if merely by thinking, we cause our internal chemistry to be nudged out of normal range so often that the body's self-regulation system finally redefines these abnormal states as normal, regular states? If this is the case, then what are the implications?

It's possible that up until now, we just haven't given this issue as much attention as it deserves.

An Experiment in the Mind-Body Connection

Now it's time for you to pay attention and sharpen your awareness: Is it the sound of the freezer or refrigerator?

Do you hear the sound of a car going by your house? A 24 dog barking in the distance? What about the way the rhythm of your own heartbeat resonates within you?

Simply by shifting your attention during those brief moments, you generated a power surge and voltage flux of electricity in millions of brain cells located right inside of your own head. You modified your brain by consciously deciding to alter your level of awareness. You not only altered the way in which your brain was functioning a few moments ago, but you also altered the way in which it will function in the next moment and maybe for the rest of your life.

By focusing your attention on these sounds, you have caused a change in the amount of blood that flows to various portions of your brain. You have also kicked off a chain reaction of impulses, which re-routes and modifies the electrical currents that are going to various parts of the brain. On a microscopic scale, a myriad of distinct nerve cells banded together chemically in order to "hold hands" and interact with one another in the interest of establishing stronger connections that will last for a longer period of time.

Your brain, which is a shimmering three-dimensional web of delicate neurological tissue, is firing in novel combinations and sequences because of the shift in attention that you are currently focusing on. You accomplished that of your own free will by shifting your attention to a different subject.

As human beings, we have the innate capacity to concentrate our attention on any topic that we choose. As we are going to discover in this book, the way in which and where we direct our focus, as well as the object of that focus and the length of time we direct it toward that object, eventually identify us on a neurological level. It is where and on what we focus our attention that determines the very trajectory of our state of being at any given moment.

If you focus your attention on a painful sensation in your body, it will become more real. This is because the neural pathways in your brain that are responsible for the experience of pain will become electrically active when you do so. The neural circuits in the brain that are responsible for processing pain and other physical sensations can be literally turned off when the focus of our awareness is shifted away from the source of the pain; as a result, the discomfort is alleviated. However, when we check to see if the pain is gone for good, the brain circuits that are associated with that pain become activated, causing us to experience the anguish once again.

In addition, the strength of the connections between these brain circuits is increased if they are repeatedly activated. Therefore, by paying attention to pain on a regular basis, we are wiring ourselves neuronally to acquire a more acute awareness of pain perception. This is because the relevant brain circuits grow more enriched as a result of our continued focus on pain.

If we think about a sour memory from our past that is permanently etched in the nooks and crannies of the gray matter of our brains, we can bring it back to life at any time by simply thinking about it. It's almost like magic.

We also have the option of attending to anxieties and worries about the future, which do not readily exist until they are conjured up by our own minds and brought into existence. However, we consider them to be real.

Everything comes to life when we pay attention to it, and things that were before overlooked or unreal become tangible through this process.

This is one possible explanation as to why we are defined by our experiences of suffering, as well as memories from our distant past. What we think about on a regular basis, and the places in which we concentrate our attention, shape who we are on a neurological level. The field of neuroscience has now come to the realization that the focused attention that is repeatedly directed toward any one topic can mold and form the neurological architecture that underpins the self.

CHAPTER 3

Beliefs in Your Mind Can Influence

Actions in Your Body

When given the opportunity, your mind can be an extremely effective therapeutic tool. Both the brain and the rest of the body contain thousands of naturally occurring chemicals. Our very own brains contain a mind-boggling variety of chemical substances that have curative properties, and our minds can influence the production and release of these substances.

When you have a strong belief in something, your brain will typically produce certain chemicals that will cause the experience you have come to expect. This is the basis of the "placebo effect." In this chapter, we discuss the placebo effect as an example to show how beliefs in your mind can influence and control physical processes and actions in your body.

What Is the "Placebo Effect?"

The concept that one's mind can trick their body into believing that a therapy is effective when it is not has been around for millennia. This concept is known as the placebo effect. When someone imagines that a specific substance has healing properties, often, the substance actually performs the imagined actions. Now that science has done more research, it has been shown that a placebo can be just as effective as conventional treatments when certain conditions are met.

An intriguing study was carried out at the University of Turin in Italy, in which volunteers had an analgesic cream rubbed on either their left or right hand or foot (Benedetti & Piedimonte, 2019). At least, this was what they had been told. In fact, it was just an inert cream and didn't differ from any regular moisturizing lotions.

Then, the volunteers received injections of capsaicin into each of their hands or feet. Capsaicin is the chemical that causes the burning sensation that you get from eating chili peppers. When injected into the skin, it produces a painful sensation. However, in the participants of the study, the pain level was significantly reduced on the hand to which the placebo cream had been administered but not on the hand to which the cream had not been applied. For instance, if the cream was rubbed into their left hand but not their right hand, the pain was significantly mitigated in their left hand but not in their right.

The researchers then studied the production of natural painkillers in the volunteers' brains using sophisticated methods. When a person receives a real painkiller, the brain makes its own natural painkillers, called endogenous opiates. The brains of the participants in this study produced their own natural painkillers in the same way. Surprisingly, however, the opiates were only created in the part of the brain that corresponded to the hand that had been touched with the placebo cream. If the cream was massaged on the person's left hand, the portion of the person's brain that controls their left hand would release endogenous opiates, whereas the region that controls their right hand would not.

These findings indicate that there was a selective and targeted placebo effect in the portion of the body that the volunteers were focused on or expected pain relief from.

Regardless of whether it was the left or right hand, the brain made its own natural painkillers in that particular region and not in any other regions of the brain (Benedetti & Piedimonte, 2019).

There are still some gaps in our understanding of how placebos work, but we do know that it involves a complex neurobiological reaction. This reaction involves an increase in feel-good neurotransmitters, such as endorphins and dopamine, as well as an increase in activity in certain brain regions that are linked to moods, emotional reactions, and self-awareness. These changes have the potential to be beneficial to the therapeutic treatment. The placebo effect is your brain's way of communicating with your body, telling it what it needs to do to feel better.

However, the release of brainpower is not the only effect that a placebo has. You also need to go through the motions of the treatment. When you look at these studies that compare real drugs to fake ones, you'll notice that there are other factors at play, such as the setting and procedures. You are required to check in at a clinic at certain intervals and submit to examinations carried out by personnel dressed in white coats. You are given a wide variety of unusual medicines and subjected to several peculiar treatments. Because you feel that you are getting attention and care, all of this can have a significant impact on how your body interprets the sensations that it is experiencing.

How Does the Placebo Effect Happen?

In 1978, researchers at the University of California, San Francisco, demonstrated for the first time that the brain produces its own natural painkillers when a person takes a placebo (Levine, 1978). Placebo analgesia refers to the phenomenon in which a person experiences relief from pain after taking a sugar pill, which is intended to fake the effects of a real medication. It was discovered that the brain produces opiate substances similar to morphine, but rather than being synthetic versions of morphine, they were the body's own naturally occurring opiates, or endogenous opiates.

More recent research is beginning to reveal that the same type of reaction occurs when placebos are given for a wide variety of diseases (Haour, 2005). Namely, after taking the placebo, the brain develops a natural 'drug' that delivers the effects that the individual anticipates would occur. The brain actually responds in a meaningful way to placebo therapies. The belief that a treatment will be successful can stimulate the release of neurotransmitters, the synthesis of hormones, and immunological responses, which can alleviate the symptoms of painful conditions, inflammatory diseases, and mood disorders.

Brain Imaging Reveals Brain Response to Placebo

Experiments that use brain imaging reveal that the brain has a real response to the expectations and circumstances around placebos. This response can have an effect on the body. Let's have a look at how researchers have cracked the mystery of how the brain responds to placebo in order to alleviate pain.

A number of experiments have been conducted that were similar to this one: in order to alleviate the participants' discomfort, two distinct lotions are applied, one to each participant's arm. They are informed that one of the treatments is a potent pain reliever, but the other won't have any impact. In fact, they are both the same cream that does not contain any analgesic ingredients.

Afterward, a stimulus that is only moderately unpleasant is administered to patients' arms, and real-time imaging of the patients' brains are performed so that researchers can observe how the patients' brains react to the sensation of pain.

It has been shown that some parts of a patient's brain light up more when they are given a placebo medication for their pain (Kong et al., 2007). One of these is the prefrontal cortex, which is a part of the brain that is responsible for higher-level thinking and has the ability to incorporate context information around a placebo, such as a confident doctor wearing a white coat or the sensation of physically administering a medicine. After that, the prefrontal cortex is able to connect to other parts of the brain that are responsible for the production of neurochemicals, such as dopamine (which indicates pleasure), oxytocin (sometimes known as the "cuddle hormone"), and opioids. These opioids have a powerful effect that is both soothing and anti-pain.

The administration of the placebo causes an increase in all of these neurochemicals, which, in turn, causes the periaqueductal gray region of the brain to produce an even greater quantity of opioids. Finally, these neurochemicals send a signal down to the spinal cord that says, "Hey! The pain has been alleviated!"

Placebo effects can also function in the opposite direction. This occurs through a reduction in the activity of pathways flowing from the spinal cord upward, which are the pathways that initially signal body pain to the brain.

After receiving a placebo treatment, the brain is also able to regulate other processes, such as the synthesis of hormones and even immune reactions. In each of these instances, researchers have identified a centrally situated and very small area of the brain, known as the hypothalamus, as being implicated (Wager & Atlas, 2015).

Multiple objective measurements demonstrate that the brain responds to placebos, and thus, it truly affects the body. But still a lot more research has to be done in order to fully understand the placebo effect. For example, why does the brain react to placebos? Is it possible that the brain finds it beneficial to instantly boost body processes in order to get a head start on solving a problem?

In addition, researchers are currently investigating why some people are more prone to the effects of placebos than others. This disparity may be the result of individual variances in the production and metabolism of neurochemicals in the brain.

This is an example of mind over the body on the molecular level. It is no longer acceptable to dismiss the placebo effect as a fabrication of people's imagination or something that is "all in the mind," as it is commonly referred to. We now know that changes in mental activity can actually result in biochemical changes in the body.

Techniques That Enhance the Placebo Effect

Various techniques can be used to enhance the effect of beliefs in the mind on the body.

These techniques involve conditioning, perception, and culture.

The Power of Conditioning

Conditioning is one method that can be used to increase the effectiveness of a placebo. When conducting a conditioning experiment on a patient, researchers will typically give them a real drug for a couple of days. Then, they switch the patients, without their knowledge, over to a placebo on the third day of the experiment. Naturally, the patient has no reason to suspect anything. As a result, when they receive their 'medicine' (the placebo), they anticipate experiencing the same degree of relief as they did while they were taking the real treatment. They have been "conditioned" to believe that the injection or tablet will continue to be effective.

According to studies, the effect is greater, the longer the conditioning is carried out. In a few of the conditioning tests, the placebo effect was amplified to the point where it affected a very high percentage of the participants; this means that almost everybody was influenced (Bräscher et al., 2018).

Scientists conducted an experiment in which they offered healthy volunteers a flavored beverage that contained a substance known as cyclosporine A, which inhibits the immune system (Kirchhof et al., 2018). The immune systems of the volunteers continually declined as a result of drinking the beverage. Even after the scientists switched out the drink for one that did not contain any cyclosporine A after a few days, the volunteers continued to develop compromised immune systems. If the researchers had given the patients a placebo drink on the first day of the experiment and warned them that it would lower their immune systems, the experiment may not have had as significant of an impact.

Conditioning enhances the effectiveness of placebos as well as the power of the mind; it enables us to change systems in the body that we normally would not be able to change. It demonstrates, quite clearly, that our minds have a significant amount of power to exert influence over our bodies. We simply have to find ways to harness that power.

The Influence of Perception

If a person is given a gigantic machine that shoots out lightning bolts as a treatment for an ailment, and the machine is portrayed as the most advanced healing system ever, then it will probably perform better than a tablet–even if the machine and tablet are both essentially placebos. It is not the machine or tablet themselves that heal, but rather how we perceive them to be doing so. It is for this reason that placebos are more effective if they have a pungent medicinal odor, are packaged in brown bottles, have a name that sounds scientific, or even if they are unpleasant or invasive.

Brand-name medications that appear to be more expensive function significantly better than generic alternatives. Even though they are both placebos, the one that seems more costly works better than the cheaper-looking one. There are even instances in which there is not that much of a difference in the effectiveness of an expensive placebo and inexpensive real medicine.

An illustration of this would be what takes place with paracetamol. Compared to the cheaper, plain, and mass-produced tablets that are sold in supermarkets, branded tablets, which have a distinctive shape and packaging, appear to be more effective for the people. It is evidently the brand, price (which was almost ten times more), appearance, and packaging of the tablets that give people more faith in the branded alternatives than they had in plain generic pain relievers.

People may perceive the tablets sold in mass markets to be of lower quality and less potent; and because of this perception, they may be less effective, even though they contain the same active ingredient. The names given to medications by their manufacturers in the pharmaceutical industry are frequently chosen to increase the drug's perceived effect.

The Influence of Culture

Because the culture in which we were raised shapes our worldview, the strength of the placebo effect varies greatly from one person to the next. In a study conducted in the United States on treatments for migraines, it was shown that placebo injections were around 50% more effective than placebo tablets (de Craen et al., 2000). On the other hand, things are quite different in Europe.

There, patients with the same disease who took placebo tablets fared about 10% better than those who received placebo injections.

According to researchers, "getting a shot" is far more common in the United States, which leads people to believe in it more; as a result, a placebo injection works better in the United States (de Craen et al., 2000).

However, people in Europe are known to "pop pills," and, as a result, a placebo tablet is more likely to be effective there.

CHAPTER 4

Visualize What You Want

This world is but a canvas to our imagination. –Henry David Thoreau

The fact that the word "imagination" bears the root of the word "magic" is certainly not a coincidence.

Imagination's operations are shrouded in mystery and appear to defy logic as they take place deep within the interior world of the human psyche. It has the potential to motivate you to investigate the innumerable opportunities that life presents, assist you at each stage of the journey toward achieving your objectives, and serve as a springboard for creative endeavors of any kind.

In fact, imagination possesses the power to form every single aspect of one's life.

The Power of Imagination

It doesn't matter how you use your imagination. You can employ visualization and affirmations or try your hand at self-hypnosis; the fact remains that your imagination has the power to alter your mental, emotional, and behavioral patterns. This makes it a great resource for bringing about a wide variety of positive changes in your life.

Even though the fact that making use of one's imagination as a means of achieving their goals is not a novel concept, it wasn't until the 20th century that specific methods were established to employ the imagination as a tool for personal development. Through the practice of visualization and affirmations, as well as through an awareness of metaphysical laws such as the well-known Law of Attraction, authors of self-help books have motivated a large number of individuals to make healthy and substantial changes in their lives.

Imagination is an internal resource that can be drawn upon in every aspect of life. It is a resource that, utilized correctly, has the capacity to define who you are, how you choose to live, and what you offer to the world. If you use your imagination wisely, it has the power to shape all of these things. It has the potential to assist you in overcoming obstacles and bringing about profound levels of change, both of which are frequently necessary in order to accomplish goals.

The Use of Imagination in Healing and Pain Management

In the early 1900s, a French psychologist named Émile Coué made the discovery that patients could benefit from auto-suggestion in their healing process (Robertson, 2009). He stated that "when your desires and imagination are at odds with one another, your imagination will invariably win the day." A phrase that Coué urged his patients to say was, "Every day, in every way, I am getting better and better." This phrase helped make Coué famous. In addition to this, he devised a method in which patients were able to alleviate their pain, whether it was mental or physical, by settling their minds and repeating the phrase, "It is vanishing, it is vanishing, it is vanishing."

Visualization Can Help Boost Your Immune System

There is evidence that practicing visualization can boost immune function (Donaldson, 2000). Many people would think that the benefits are due merely to a reduction in stress while a person is practicing visualization. At first glance, this would make sense, considering that visualizing something is typically done while relaxing, and a state of relaxation can, in fact, lower stress. However, the effect of visualizing on the immune system is not just limited to its relaxing aspect.

Imagery that is geared toward the immune system has been utilized in a number of studies in an effort to demonstrate the specific effects of the practice of visualizing. The purpose of these studies was to evaluate the effectiveness of a relaxing visualization versus a more targeted visualization of the immune system.

Immune System-Targeted Imagery

One study used imagery in an effort to boost the white blood cell (WBC) counts of 20 patients (10 males and 10 females) who had lowered WBC counts as a result of their illnesses (Donaldson, 2000). The participant suffered from illnesses such as cancer, AIDS, viral infections, sinusitis, endometriosis, allergies, hepatitis, and a variety of other diseases. The WBC counts of the patients in question had been persistently lower than the usual anticipated range for at least six months.

This investigation lasted for several months. The WBC counts continued to decrease after the study began. This trend continued for five days, but then patients' WBC count experienced a considerable increase over the subsequent three months, as assessed by a 17% increase after one month, 31% increase after two months, and 38% increase after three months.

Based on the evidence that has been presented throughout this book, as well as the studies that you will read about in the following section–where immune system-targeted visualization has been used by cancer patients in randomized controlled trials–it appears that visualization has a genuinely beneficial effect on the immune system.

Given that the immune system is the primary system in our body responsible for repairing damage caused by injury, illness, and disease, the phenomenon has enormous repercussions. If positive changes in immune function can be brought about by visualization, then it stands to reason that this practice may have the capacity to affect a wide variety of medical issues as a complement to medical treatment.

There is little doubt that mental status can have an effect on one's physical health. The results of recent studies make it abundantly evident that one's state of mind can have a direct influence on their immune system. It is possible that with additional research and experience, we will be able to learn skills that can help us maintain our health significantly better by optimizing our immune systems. Alternatively, we may be able to develop ways that, in conjunction with medical treatment, can specifically target different systems of the body in order to speed up recovery from injury, illness, and disease.

Visualization Can Help in the Fight Against Cancer

Research has been done that applies the concept of imagining the immune system to patients who have cancer. In a randomized controlled trial, which was published in the journal *Breast*, researchers asked women who were undergoing treatment (chemotherapy, surgery, radiation, and hormone treatment) for newly-diagnosed, locally-advanced breast cancer to also make use of visualization (Eremin et al., 2009).

The participants were randomly divided into two groups.

The first group imagined their immune systems eliminating the cancer cells, but the other half did not.

The first group of women were shown cartoons that portrayed the process of the immune system fighting cancer cells, but they were also encouraged to create their own images in their heads. On a scale from 1 to 10, they ranked the degree to which their visualizations were clear. Over the course of weeks, blood samples were drawn and analyzed 10 times, and a variety of immunological components were examined.

When compared with the women who didn't imagine, the immunological activity levels of the women who did visualize were much higher. Specifically, the levels of T-cells, activated T-cells, and lymphokine-activated killer cells in the blood of individuals who visualized were higher than average. In addition, the women who reported the highest levels of visualization clarity also had significantly greater levels of natural killer cell activity not only during treatment, but also after treatment and again during follow-up.

The researchers found that using guided imagery had a positive effect on potential anticancer host defenses both during and after receiving medical and surgical treatment. In several other investigations, researchers observed the same trend of increased immune system activation when visualization was employed in conjunction with cancer treatment (Case et al., 2018).

To be clear, visualization was not utilized in place of conventional medical treatment; rather, it was used in conjunction with conventional treatment. Visualization is something that we do in addition to treatment, not in place of it; just as we don't meditate in place of sleeping but rather in addition to it, and meditation has a tendency to improve the quality of our sleep. In a similar vein, these investigations on cancer showed that the process of visualizing one's condition tended to improve the efficacy of the treatment by bolstering the activity of the immune system.

Visualization for Mitigating the Adverse Effects of Chemotherapy

Researchers have investigated whether the practice of visualization can help persons with cancer better manage their symptoms and the adverse effects of their therapy.

Studies have shown that guided imagery can help patients suffering from a variety of illnesses, including cancer, with their levels of pain, exhaustion, tension, anxiety, despair, and sleep, as well as speed up their recovery time. Additionally, it can lessen adverse effects, such as nausea and vomiting, that may be brought on by chemotherapy and the discomfort that is experienced during procedures.

In 2016, researchers investigated the effects of guided imagery and progressive muscle relaxation (Charalambous et al., 2016). They were curious as to whether it could assist in alleviating symptoms such as fatigue, discomfort, nausea, vomiting, anxiety, and depression. Participants in the study were going through chemotherapy for various cancers, including breast and prostate cancer.

They discovered that those who participated in the relaxation techniques had an improvement in their symptoms. The research did have several shortcomings, and additional investigation is required; however, the researchers think that these methods of relaxing might be beneficial for those who are undergoing treatment for cancer.

Visualization to Enhance Mood and Life Quality

Visualization can be a very helpful tool for cancer patients who are looking for ways to deal with the emotional toll that their disease takes on them. According to a number of studies, the practice of visualizing positive outcomes is connected with improved levels of comfort, lower levels of anxiety, decreased levels of fear of death, and decreased levels of mental problems (Nguyen & Brymer, 2018). As mentioned before, the use of visualization is not intended to take the place of conventional medical treatment.

An analysis of six clinical trials published in 2005 revealed that guided imagery might be effective in assisting persons with cancer in the management of stress, anxiety, and depression (Roffe et al., 2005). There is a need for additional research in this area.

Researchers investigated the effects of meditation, breathing exercises, muscular relaxation, and visual imagery (Lindquist et al., 2013). The researchers built a tool kit to test if these strategies could lower anxiety prior to and following surgery for breast cancer. They came to the conclusion that the relaxation techniques helped some of the participants in the study. It helped them emotionally, which in turn helped them be more resilient to the effects of cancer treatment. More research, preferably on a more extensive scale, is required.

Types of Visualization

Visualization can take different forms from creative visualization to guided imagery. Let's take a closer look at these modalities of visualization.

Creative Visualization

The widely practiced method of creative visualization is based on the idea that one's imagination may play a significant part in the process of bringing about desirable outcomes in one's life. In creative visualization, you form mental images depicting how you would like things to be.

It requires you to bring these optimistic mental images into your mind's eye on a consistent basis, which in turn sends a consistent message to your subconscious mind that you expect to achieve your objective. Creative visualization can be utilized in this way as a highly successful method for goal attainment. It can be used to better one's profession, relationships, health, or any other aspect of their life.

One of the most significant benefits of visualization is that it enables you to conjure up emotions and thoughts connected to events that you might not even have had.

Because the subconscious mind is incapable of distinguishing between genuine and imagined experiences, the formation of mental images can effectively serve as the foundation of a memory bank that can be accessed whenever necessary. Therefore, creative visualization enables you to build a sense of the reality you would like to have in your life, allowing you to circumvent the rational and critical faculties of the conscious mind.

Although visuals seen in the mind's eye are the primary component of creative visualization, almost all of our senses can be employed in the process. In this way, in order to create a particularly vivid experience in your mind, in addition to the visual images you are conjuring up, you can try to imagine certain sounds, aromas, a sense of touch, and even certain tastes if they are relevant. Incorporating a sentiment or emotional component also works wonders; for instance, you could concentrate on the sensation of inner calm, thankfulness, or inspiration.

Guided Imagery

Have you ever been in the middle of a difficult situation and wished you could be somewhere else, like on a luxury cruise? If so, you are not alone. The practice of guided imagery encourages the use of one's imagination in order to transport oneself to a more relaxed and tranquil state.

Because of the close connection that exists between the mind and body, guided imagery has the power to make you feel as though you are experiencing something simply by visualizing it.

Imagine that you are experiencing an intense form of food cravings that are constructed from memory, and then you notice that your salivary glands are becoming active. An image that you have created in your thoughts and that has engaged all of your senses is causing a connection to form between your body and mind.

Imagine for a moment that you could duplicate that for the purpose of relieving pain and reducing stress.

How to Engage in Guided Imagery?

If you would like to give guided imagery a try, the following procedures need to be taken:

- Find somewhere to sit down or lie down that is comfortable, and close your eyes.

- To assist you in relaxing, you should begin by taking a few long, slow breaths.
- Imagine yourself in a place that is serene and unruffled. This might be a scene that you choose, such as a meadow, mountain setting, or any other scenario.
- Imagine the scene, and make an effort to include some specifics. Consider this: What does the sky look like? Is the sky clear or are there clouds? Is there a breeze blowing? How does it feel?
- Including a walkway in your scenario might frequently be of assistance. Imagine that as you step onto a beach, you venture into the sea and feel the relaxing sensation of water on your skin. As you wade in the water, you will begin to experience a growing sense of calmness and joy.
- When you are completely immersed in your scenario and begin to feel at ease, take a few minutes to slow your breathing and become aware of the serenity around you.
- Think of a simple word or sound that you can use at a later time to guide you back to this location.

  You can utilize this in the future.
- Then, when you feel you are ready, carefully bring yourself back to the here and now from the situation you were just in. Tell yourself that you will feel rested and rejuvenated and that you will carry your sense of serenity with you as you go about your day.
- Count to three and open your eyes. Take note of how you are currently feeling.

It could be helpful to have a guide or audio recording to follow along with. You can also use a set of written instructions or a script, but listening to the instructions may be a better method to ease into the process and become comfortable with it.

What Is the Difference Between Creative Visualization and Guided Imagery?

How is guided imagery different from creative visualization? When a person concentrates their attention solely on sights, they are said to be visualizing.

While in guided imagery, you are encouraged to make use of all of your senses, including sight, taste, hearing, smell, and touch, in order to create mental images that your body experiences as being just as real as actual occurrences in the outside world. This is in contrast to more traditional visualization, which focuses solely on the mental state without the addition of whole-body senses.

This does not mean that during the practice, you will be seeing, smelling, or tasting things in your real physical body, but rather that your mind will be visualizing the components that make up each sense. Because of the very physical connection that exists between the mind and body, the practice of guided imagery can actually promote changes in the patterns of one's heart rate, blood pressure, and breathing.

What makes guided imagery distinct from hypnosis?

Hypnosis, in almost all cases, calls for the involvement of both a subject and hypnotist. The hypnotist makes suggestions to the subject so that they can more easily access the participant's subconscious mind. Through the use of guided imagery, you are putting the full power of your imagination to work for you.

CHAPTER 5

Unleash the Power of Self-Affirmation

Self-affirmation is another example of the amazing powers the mind has over the body. Self-affirmative statements can be helpful in keeping one's attention on one's goal for wellness. However, in order to make use of self-affirmation to enhance your health, you must first understand what this practice is.

What Is Self-Affirmation?

The power of words should not be underestimated. Self-affirmations are positive remarks that are brief, simple, and easy to grasp. The sentences are stated in the present tense, whether they are spoken or written. As long as you make sure to say them the right way and do so on a consistent basis, they have the potential to perform wonders for you in terms of assisting you in achieving your wellness goals.

The purpose of self-affirmations is to break you out of any negative thought patterns that may be building in your head at the time. As a direct result of this, they make it easier for you to conquer mental health issues, such as anxiety, depression, and others, and help you develop new ways of thinking that are geared toward positivity, inspiration, and motivation.

People have a tendency to be overly critical of themselves, which can cause them to lose motivation when they are working out or reach a hurdle on the path toward improved health.

Affirmations stop you from "falling further down the rabbit hole" of negativity, which would otherwise be destructive.

The field of psychology has been making use of affirmations of one's own worth for quite some time. It is generally agreed that Claude Steele (1988), a well-known psychologist in the United States, is the person who first coined the term "self-affirmation," which is critical to our current comprehension of the topic. According to Steele's idea, an individual needs to uphold a certain perspective of oneself. For instance, they may have a self-perception that they are moral, knowledgeable, powerful, or capable individuals. People are able to more effectively continue on their journey to become happier, healthier, and better individuals in general when they engage in self-affirmation.

According to Steele, "psychological discomfort" occurs in people whenever the external world forces them to reconsider how they see themselves. In today's terminology, we may refer to this as depression, anxiety, or any other of the several mental health problems that are out there.

According to Steele, practicing self-affirmation does not mean perceiving ourselves to be flawless beings. It is about reinforcing our connection to certain ideals while concentrating on the things that we care deeply about and hold in high regard (1988).

Scientific Research Shows the Effectiveness of Self-affirmation

Neuroscientific research has been conducted to investigate whether there are any changes in the brain when positive self-affirmations are made. There is data gathered from MRIs suggesting that specific brain pathways become more active when people engage in self-affirmation (Cascio et al., 2015). More specifically, when we think about our personal values, greater activity is generated in the ventromedial prefrontal cortex of the brain. This part of the brain is involved in the positive evaluation and processing of information connected to the self.

The following is an example of data from a scientific study that demonstrates how the engagement of positive self-affirmation can be advantageous:

Self-affirmations have been shown to decrease health-damaging stress (Critcher & Dunning, 2014). They may help us to perceive otherwise "threatening" messages with less resistance. Self-affirmations can make us less likely to dismiss harmful health messages, responding instead with the intention to improve our health.

How to Practice Affirmative Self-Talk?

Self-affirmations are words that call us to action. You will obtain the most benefit possible from them if you are consistent and do not give up. There are certain people who practice them frequently. Others participate in self-affirmation on an as-needed basis or whenever they could use a "pick-me-up" in terms of their level of vitality.

Affirmations about one's health are at their most powerful when they are uttered loudly, stated in the present tense, and accompanied by a good frame of mind.

Some people find it enjoyable to say self-affirmative words to themselves when they are working out. They are helped in returning to their centers and are reminded of the value of the activity they are doing by the affirmations. It is a powerful exercise in re-orienting one's perspective.

Some people find it beneficial to utter health affirmations out loud before or during their meditation sessions in order to more firmly plant their thoughts in the present time. If you want to use health affirmations in a way that is empowering and healing, you can say them to yourself in front of a mirror. When you stare in the mirror and make eye contact with yourself, the efficacy of your affirmations is significantly increased.

Imagine that you are communicating with yourself through these words and that their energy is enabling you to be purified, healed, and supported in some way. When you undertake this practice for the very first time, you may find that you are overcome with sensations of embarrassment, compulsion, and inauthenticity, but carry on and say them whether you mean it or not.

Negative mental self-talk that has been going on for decades cannot be changed in a single night. By maintaining your practice, you are not only learning to rebuild the way in which you regard yourself, but also learning how to be appreciative of who you are. This is a significantly important advantage of health affirmations.

Self-Affirmations for You

The following is a list of powerful health affirmations that you can choose from to improve your mental, as well as physical, health:

- I am strong.
- I am confident.
- I am growing better and better every day.
- I am excited about the day ahead.

- I can find everything that I require within me right now.
- I am an irresistible force of nature that cannot be stopped.
- I am a walking, talking illustration of the power of motivation.
- I am enjoying a life filled with plenty.
- I am able to motivate and encourage others.
- I am elevating myself above the thoughts that are attempting to provoke anger or fear in me.

  This day is amazing in every way.
- I am cranking up the volume on the positive things in my life while simultaneously turning down the volume on the negative things.
- I am able to concentrate quite well.
- I am not driven by my challenges; rather, I am guided by my aspirations.
- I want to express my gratitude for everything that has been given to me in my life.
- I am not dependent on anyone else and can support myself.
- I am free to become whatever and whoever I want to be.
- My history does not determine who I am; rather, it is what lies ahead that motivates me.
- The day ahead will be one filled with accomplishments.
- I am able to concentrate.
- Every single day, I have a deeper sense of gratitude.
- Every day, I make progress toward becoming healthier.

- My progress toward accomplishing my objectives continues to accelerate day by day.
- Incredible shifts are taking place in me and my life at this very moment as a direct result of the power of the ideas and words I have been thinking and speaking.
- I am always learning new things and becoming a more well-rounded individual as a result.
- I am overcoming all of the damaging fears and doubts that have been holding me back.
- I make peace within my mind and heart by accepting myself exactly as I am.
- I am going to pardon my past mistakes and set myself free. I deserve to forgive and be forgiven.
- Every day, I make progress in my mending and strengthening.

  I've been through challenging moments in the past, and the only thing that's come out of them is that they've made me stronger and better. I'm going to go through this unscathed. I just know it.
- Not a single day of my life is wasted away by me in any way.
- Today, tomorrow, and every day that I have left on this planet, I wring every last drop of worthiness out of the experience.
- I have to keep in mind the amazing power that resides within me so that I can accomplish everything my heart desires.
- When I find myself in a scenario, or with a person that isn't beneficial for my well-being, I remove myself from the unhealthy environment or person.

- I don't interact with people who try to implant detrimental ideas and concepts in my head.
- I am not an outsider in this world; there are people that recognize and appreciate what I bring to the table.
- Even though I have a dark history, I am still an attractive person.
- I recognize that I am not perfect, but I refuse to let my shortcomings determine who I am.
- The warmth of my spirit emanates from within and spreads to the spirits of others around me.
- The only person I can accurately compare myself to is the version of myself that existed the day before. And as long as the person I am today is even the least bit better than the person I was yesterday, I will have achieved what I consider to be a successful outcome according to my own standards.
- I focus on finishing what is important to me and letting go of the rest.
- I satisfy the hunger in my soul. I train my body.
- Right now is my turn.
- Meaning can be found in my life. The things that I do have significance.
- The work I've done today represents the pinnacle of my abilities in that regard.
- To that end, I express my gratitude.
- Just one upbeat idea first thing in the morning can completely transform my day. Therefore, I will start

today with a strong idea in order to establish the tone for the day and pave the way for success to reverberate through every moment of the next 24 hours.

- I make plans for the future and pursue those plans with every ounce of grit that I possess. When I do this, my own skills and abilities will take me to locations that I would never have imagined being possible.
- Being happy is a choice, and I've made that decision for myself today.

CHAPTER 6

The Power of Positive Thinking

A pessimist sees the difficulty in every opportunity; an optimist sees the opportunity in every difficulty.–

Winston Churchill

A 447-person, 30-year study carried out by researchers at the Mayo Clinic in the United States found that pessimists die younger than optimists do (Giltay et al., 2004). In this chapter, we will discuss this finding and other evidence for the amazing power of positive thinking on health.

The Surprising Effects of Positive Thinking on Your Health

Positive thinking can have various powerful effects on health. In this chapter, we explore these health effects.

The Power of Optimism and the Secret to Long Life

Pessimists tend to have shorter lifespans than optimists.

This was the conclusion reached by a study that was published in the academic journal, *Archives of General Psychiatry* (Giltay et al., 2004). The researchers came to the conclusion that there is a "protective relationship between optimism and all-cause mortality in old age."

Optimists were discovered to have fewer physical and emotional health problems, less discomfort, higher energy, and a general sense of being more serene, happier, and calmer than pessimists.

Being optimistic guards against getting sick. The responses of 999 Dutch men and women between the ages of 65 and 85 to a variety of phrases were analyzed by the researchers, including:

- I feel that life is full of promises.
- I have optimistic aspirations for my future.
- Most of the time, I am filled with joy.
- I frequently have joyous laughter.
- There are still a lot of things I want to do.
- I have a mostly positive attitude.

The findings were striking: Those participants who responded affirmatively to the questions and reported high levels of optimism had a 45% reduced risk of death from any cause and 77% lower risk of death from heart disease than those participants who reported high levels of pessimism.

The Power of Positive Thinking and the Immune System

To a large extent, a person's frame of mind determines their emotional experience, that is, whether they respond to the challenges of life with more positive or negative feelings. One of the many reasons why maintaining a happy attitude is so vital is that it has the potential to strengthen our immune system and, as a result, our capacity to ward off illness.

Our attitudes toward the various challenges we face in life influence how we respond to those problems. Having a positive attitude makes it easier for us to deal with difficult situations and even enables us to identify opportunities in the difficulties we face, which is ultimately beneficial to our health.

In a study that was carried out at Carnegie Mellon University in the United States, researchers investigated the effects that influenza and common cold viruses had on individuals who exhibited a variety of emotional types (Cohen et al., 2006). A total of 193 healthy volunteers were asked to identify whether they had positive, happier emotions or negative emotional style (unfavorable emotions).

The results of the study showed that the majority of the volunteers had a positive emotional style. After that, they were given nasal drops containing viruses. It was shown that individuals who had a higher frequency of positive emotions had a much lower incidence of upper respiratory infections than individuals who had a higher frequency of negative emotions.

As we journey through life, the attitudes we hold influence how we respond to infections caused by bacteria, viruses, and other pathogens. The ability to have a constructive perspective on life is eventually beneficial to one's overall health and lifespan.

Thinking Optimistically and the Heart

One of the most well-studied impacts of attitude is its influence on the cardiovascular system. Researchers at the Duke University Medical Center (2003) in North Carolina discovered, through an examination of people with heart disease, that those patients who routinely felt more positive emotions (such as happiness, joy, and optimism) had approximately a 20% greater chance of being alive 11 years later than those who experienced more negative emotions.

In a separate study, researchers looked at the correlation between aggressive personality qualities and coronary artery calcification in middle-aged and older married couples

(Smith et al., 2007). According to the findings of the study, researchers discovered that a hostile attitude is linked to concurrent coronary artery disease.

Strategies to Nurture Positive Thinking in Your Life

It's not only the things that occur to us during our lives that determine the state of our health and happiness. The most important thing is how we react to it. The good news is that we are able to alter our mentality. If we dig deep inside ourselves, we can always select the option that is the most morally superior, comes from the kindest heart, contributes to the comfort and happiness of other people, and the choice that, as a result, improves our own physical health.

They say that attitude is important, and the statement contains a great deal of truth. If we can train ourselves to look on the bright side of situations, we will likely enjoy longer, healthier, and more fulfilled lives. Stopping the whining, practicing more gratitude, and being more generous are effective methods for achieving this goal.

Put an End to Complaining

Many of us have made complaining about circumstances and criticizing others into a way of life, and, most of the time, we aren't even aware of how frequently we engage in these behaviors. Yet, when we complain, it is almost never about the facts themselves, but rather how they appear to us. One person's interpretation of the same thing could be entirely different from another's.

Consider the scenario in which a delivery that you were anticipating does not arrive. You gripe about how this has destroyed your day and thrown off your entire schedule, and you call it a delay. You put unnecessary strain on yourself, which has a wide range of adverse repercussions on your health. Someone else who is waiting on a late delivery may come to the conclusion that there is something else they could be doing in the meanwhile, and that they will ultimately find that the delay was for the best. Should we look at the delay as a positive or negative development? That is up to you to decide. However, the choices you make have an impact on your well-being.

Complaining has an effect on not only us but also the people around us. We don't give it much thought, but we're a lot like tuning forks. When you strike the fork, objects and events in the immediate vicinity resonate with it. Complaining loudly and frequently in the presence of other people has a negative effect and causes them to start complaining as well. It would appear that, all of a sudden, they too are motivated to find fault with life and everything around them. Complaining transforms into an emotional virus that we take with us wherever we go, infecting the people who we come into contact with along the way.

Our thoughts and attitudes serve as a push for our actions, and our actions serve as the primary factor in the formation of our world. Therefore, the world around us is a product of our thoughts and attitudes. What kind of world would you choose to live in? If we refrain from griping about the state of the world, we will be able to concentrate on making it a better place. At the same time, we are contributing favorably to the wellbeing of our bodies by engaging in this activity.

Try to shift your attention away from your grievances and onto the things for which you are thankful. Gratitude generates gratitude. The more things that you concentrate on that you are thankful for, the more things you will become aware of and encounter in your life for which you might be grateful. In doing so, you are benefiting your health.

Be Kind to Each Other

Spending money on other people brings you greater enjoyment than spending money on yourself, contrary to the natural inclination of many individuals. According to a body of research, those who devote a greater proportion of their income to donating to charitable organizations, or giving to others, report higher levels of happiness compared to those who spend their entire income on themselves (Park et al., 2017). And we haven't even begun to consider how much joy it brings to the person who receives it.

But why? Why is it that giving to others, often known as prosocial spending, makes us feel better about ourselves?

One reason for this is that helping other people tends to make us feel better about ourselves. It contributes to the development of an image of ourselves as people who are responsible and generous, which, in turn, makes us feel pleased. Moreover, spending money on other people helps us maintain and strengthen our connections with them, which is another factor. Individuals who have stronger social bonds are, on average, happier.

Cultivate a Positive Attitude

Your mind is a very potent instrument. A positive mindset enables you to realize your greatest potential and accomplish the things you set out to do. People with a positive mental attitude have high expectations for themselves, believe they are capable of accomplishing their goals, and view obstacles as opportunities for growth.

Your capacity to adapt to changing circumstances and remain calm under pressure is enhanced when you keep a positive mental attitude. You can become more robust and improve your mental fitness by deliberately choosing to have a positive view of life. Having this mindset enables you to be more versatile and successfully navigate challenging circumstances with ease.

A person who has a positive outlook tends to see the best in people and situations. A person who has a pessimistic viewpoint, on the other hand, views the world as being full of problems. Your life's quality can be improved by cultivating a state of subjective wellbeing, which can be defined as the thought and feeling that your life is going extremely well. Additionally, it makes you a more pleasant person to be around. People have a tendency to gravitate toward those who can find happiness in the mundane aspects of life and elevate the spirits of those around them.

A more upbeat frame of mind is within our reach if we just change the way we think and behave. Listed below are some examples of how a positive attitude manifests itself in real life:

Change Your Point of View

Your outlook has a significant impact on the quality of your life and joy you experience. The ordinary activities that you carry out on a daily basis might either present you with an opportunity or burden. Let's say that this morning you are going to prepare breakfast for your family at home. This could appear to be a burdensome task at first. You had the thought, "I need to make breakfast." However, what if you rethought that situation? Start replacing phrases like "I have to" with

"I'm going to." To put it another way, try to regard the current situation as a precious gift that should be cherished. You are fortunate enough to have a family, get to spend time with them, and have food in your home.

Don't Take Things Personally

Having a positive attitude requires you to refrain from taking things to heart. The words and deeds of other people are merely a reflection of who they are as individuals. When you allow someone, or something, to affect you emotionally, you give that person power over you. Take, for example, the scenario in which you greet a coworker in the office only to be confronted with a harsh attitude in response. You make the conscious decision not to let anything insult you or cause you to harbor resentment. Instead, you choose not to take it personally.

It's possible that your coworker was having a rough day or received some disheartening news. Their demeanor was merely a manifestation of the emotions that they were experiencing.

Engage in Self-Compassion

Kindness toward oneself is as important as kindness toward one's fellow man. How you take care of yourself may be summed up in one phrase: Engage in self-care activities that boost your overall health and well-being.

For instance, make it a daily practice to boost your self-confidence by uttering positive affirmations. Saying things to yourself, like "I am proud of myself," has an effect on your subconscious mind and might help you feel better about yourself.

Be Happy for the Accomplishments of Others

People who maintain a positive mental attitude do not see themselves as competing with other individuals. They are aware that they are on their own individual path and that the accomplishments of others do not diminish the value of their own experiences. For instance, if your friend found their ideal job before you did, you should congratulate them in an authentic manner on their achievement. Your reaction to their victory should be one of motivation, not envy.

Smile! It's Contagious

People who are optimistic are more likely to have many friends and get along well with others. People are drawn to them because of the consistently pleasant mood they exude and the honesty with which they conduct themselves. For instance, a leader with a positive mental attitude will always have a grin on their face and treat their staff with respect, even if they are having a poor day themselves. Their attitude remains unaffected by the conditions that they find themselves in at the moment.

CHAPTER 7

Control Stress in Your Body Through

Your Mind

One of the most important ways the mind can affect the body is through stress. Stressful emotions and thoughts, if continued over time, can lead to an array of destructive changes in the body. You can control stress and its harmful effects on your body through your mind. If you educate yourself to be more open and less reactive, you are better equipped to cope when the stressors of life start to accumulate–whether those stressors are from work, family, relationships, school, finances, or even traffic.

Stress Can Wreak Havoc on Your Body

Stress is a natural mental and physical reaction to the events and circumstances of life. Everyone, at one point or another, will show signs of stress. Everyday responsibilities like job and family, as well as more significant life events like a new diagnosis, conflict, or the loss of a loved one, can all be sources of stress for individuals. When stress is short-lived, it can be good for your health and help you overcome challenging circumstances.

When you are stressed, your body will respond by releasing hormones that will speed up your heart rate and breathing rate, as well as get your muscles ready to react.

However, this can have a negative impact on your health if your stress response continues to activate and your levels of stress remain elevated for a much longer period of time. Long-term stress can give rise to a number of different symptoms and have an impact on your health as a whole. Irritability, anxiety, sadness, headaches, and insomnia are all examples of symptoms associated with chronic stress.

When Stress Becomes Persistent Over Time

When stress begins to interfere with your capacity to live a normal life for an extended period of time, the threat posed by it increases significantly. The longer you are under stress, the more negative effects it will have on both your mind and body. For instance, you may experience feelings of exhaustion, inability to concentrate, or irritability for no apparent reason. But prolonged exposure to stress also causes physical deterioration.

The chronic activation of the stress response system, and the excessive exposure to cortisol and other stress hormones that comes with it, can cause practically all of the functions in your body to become disrupted. This can put you at an increased risk for a wide range of physical and mental health problems, such as anxiety, depression, digestive issues, headaches, muscle tension and pain, heart disease, heart attack, high blood pressure, stroke, sleep problems, weight gain, memory and concentration impairment, and impaired sexual function.

Chronic stress may also cause disease because it leads people to engage in unhealthy coping mechanisms, such as overeating, smoking, and other poor habits. Stress at work, defined as "high demands coupled with low decision-making latitude," has been linked to an increased risk of many diseases, including cardiovascular disease (Kivimäki & Kawachi, 2015). Chronic stress also has the effect of suppressing the immune system, making it more difficult for the body to recover from sickness.

A meta-analysis conducted in 2004 examined the relationships between stress and the immune system, using data from 293 separate scientific studies (Segerstrom & Miller, 2004). It was demonstrated that stress had a detrimental effect on the immune system, which, in turn, reduces our capacity to fend off infections.

There is a strong correlation between long-term stress and a variety of different diseases. Long-term stress, for instance, has been connected with conditions such as anxiety and depression, trouble sleeping, hypertension, heart disease, stroke, cancer, ulcers, colds and flu, rheumatoid arthritis, obesity, and even the rate at which one ages (Segerstrom & Miller, 2004).

Because of this, we will be able to lead healthier lives if we are successful in lowering the amount of stress we deal with. In addition, a number of studies have demonstrated that if we reduce our levels of stress, we can recover from illness and disease more quickly.

Trying to Hide Your Stress Is an Even Worse Idea

When confronted with stressful circumstances, some people choose to communicate their thoughts and feelings to others, as well as explain the difficulties they are experiencing. Doing this can actually help them deal with the situation because they now have someone to talk to. Being honest with others acts as a release valve for their negative and overwhelming feelings. There is a saying that goes, "A problem shared is a problem halved."

Others, on the other hand, repress their emotions and don't share them with anyone because they are scared that others will criticize them or think that they aren't good enough. Sometimes they are fearful of how other people will react and believe that they will be judged.

A number of studies conducted over the course of the last few decades demonstrate that bottling up your feelings can have, and does have, an effect on both your body and mind. According to the findings of a study that was published in the *International Journal of Psychotherapy Practice and Research*, continued reliance on disguising or repressing one's emotions is a "barrier to good health" (Patel, 2019).

According to the findings of these studies, talking to other people about our issues is beneficial. It does us little benefit to bottle up our anxieties and emotional suffering inside of ourselves. The development of repressed unpleasant feelings is analogous to the expansion of a balloon within the psyche. The balloon continues to grow, and with it, the potential for disease to manifest itself in various parts of the body. We have to locate a release valve that will allow us to let out a tiny bit of the air from our stress balloons on a regular basis.

Talk About Your Worries

If your automobile breaks down, you are either able to fix it yourself or know someone who can. On the other hand, it is rather more difficult to mend broken emotions.

There is no screwdriver you can turn or a repair shop you can go to in order to get your emotions fixed. However, there is one item in your toolbox that you can always utilize, and that is talking about how you feel. Even if all you do is say out loud how you are feeling to another person, this might be beneficial. So why do we shun it or feel as though it doesn't work?

There are many different factors that contribute to why discussing our issues might be challenging. Some people, especially men, are conditioned to keep their feelings bottled up inside of them rather than express them out loud. Sometimes the feelings that you are experiencing, such as guilt over something that you did or embarrassment about how you think other people view you, can feel so overwhelming that you are unable to muster the drive to talk about it with someone else.

Talking has significant positive effects on one's mental health, some of which might not be immediately apparent. The phrase "talking about it" covers a lot of ground, so let's break it down a little bit. When we talk about talking about your concerns, there are a few different shapes that it can take:

- **Sharing Your Feelings With a Reliable Buddy:** There are instances when all that's required is to simply express how you're feeling without really formulating any solutions to the problem. You can start a conversation that will help you handle the stress after a rough day at work by saying something like, "I had the worst day at work!"
- **Having a Conversation With a Partner About a Disagreement:** Fights are inevitable in intimate relationships. However, keeping your emotions to yourself might produce problems for you and your relationship that may become worse over time.

  While it's always a good idea to work toward finding constructive solutions to the issues that have arisen in your relationship, it's also important to remember that simply opening up about your feelings with your partner can make your communication stronger.

- **Talk Therapy With a Therapist Who Is Licensed to Practice:** There's a good reason why people are willing to shell out cash only to vent their frustrations to a trained professional. Whether you need to talk about a mental illness you're battling with, are in couples counseling to work on your relationship, or just need someone to talk to who knows how to handle stress, a skilled therapist can help you hash out your feelings and address what you're going through.

Why Does Discussing It Make a Difference?

Finding a new job, severing ties with an unsuitable romantic partner, and making an effort to better oneself are all examples of actionable steps that can be taken to address issues that arise in one's personal life. But what exactly is the point of merely talking about it? When you're engaged in a grueling uphill battle against your own negative sentiments, it may seem as though talking about it is the least productive thing you can do. But talking about it can actually be very helpful. Talking actually has a number of benefits for both your body and brain.

When you are experiencing highly intense feelings, like fear, aggressiveness, or anxiety, the part of your brain, called the amygdala, is in control of how you are reacting.

It is responsible for a variety of tasks, including determining whether you should fight or run away. Your amygdala, along with the rest of the limbic system, is responsible for determining whether something poses a threat, coming up with a solution to deal with the threat if one is required, and encoding the relevant information in your memory so that you may recall it in the future.

This area of your brain has the ability to take control and even overrule more logical thought processes when you are under a lot of pressure or feeling overwhelmed.

Putting your thoughts into words, also known as "affect labeling," is a procedure that may reduce the response of the amygdala when you come into contact with items that are upsetting. In this way, you can become less bothered about something that has been annoying you. For instance, if you were involved in a car accident, even being in a car so soon after the event could cause you to feel emotionally overwhelmed. When you talk through what happened to you, put your emotions into words, and process what took place, you will find that you are able to get back into the automobile without experiencing the same emotional response.

Nothing in this should be taken to imply that talking about your issues or even participating in talk therapy with a qualified therapist would magically solve all of your problems, make you instantly happy, and restore your health. Talking can help enhance your overall wellbeing if it is combined with other health measures, such as modifying your diet and exercising regularly. Even more importantly, it can help you understand how and why you feel the way you do, which will allow you to better manage your emotions in the future.

Meditation: The Mind's Tool to Control Stress Many of us, at some point in our lives, will have had the experience of feeling overwhelmed, as if everything were simply too much to handle. Because of this, life can sometimes be very stressful.

Even while stress can have major consequences for our health, there are times when it's enough to just take a moment to stop what you're doing and give your mind a break in order to feel better in the here and now.

When practiced on a regular and consistent basis, meditation has the ability to retrain the brain in such a way that its practitioner develops a greater capacity to deal with stress. This is especially true when meditation is done daily.

The goal of meditation should not be to eliminate stress, but rather to learn how to manage it better. A significant portion of this is determined by how we react to stressful situations. If we change the way we think about something, we can reduce the negative effects on both our mental and physical health. Meditation teaches us to become witnesses to certain thought processes, and, as a result, we become less impacted by them. This allows us to be less caught up in our stress.

The negative connotations that are frequently attached to stress may not always be warranted. Consider where we would be, for instance, if we didn't have the signal of distress that tells us to get away from the impending danger. Or if we didn't feel the need to rush to complete our assignments or projects in a timely manner.

Some people are able to flourish in high-pressure occupations, where they experience a perfect sense of control when things are moving quickly but feel overwhelmed and worried when things settle down.

Therefore, the levels of stress might vary greatly from one person to the next.

The level of anxiety that we connect with a particular occurrence can actually be influenced by how we evaluate high-pressure situations. When we examine this phenomenon through the lens of attention, however, we see that it is possible to modify the manner in which we experience stress and develop a more receptive relationship to it.

Try to avoid assigning negative labels to stress when you next experience a stress response in what you would consider to be a non-dangerous situation. Instead, you should strive to think of it as something potent and invigorating that helps you get ready to face the problems that life throws at you.

Now, when things are particularly stressful, it can feel counterintuitive to sit down and do nothing; meditation can feel like the last thing we want to do at those times.

However, when we feel as though we are under a lot of strain, we are unable to think clearly. When we have too much going on, pausing what we are doing is the most effective technique to relax the mind.

Under these conditions, the purpose of meditating is to create a mental space that is more open and expansive.

And in that area, we become conscious of the tension that we are experiencing. We don't fight it or make any attempts to get rid of it. We just sit quietly and allow all of our thoughts and feelings to come to the surface. When they do, we just let them go by redirecting our focus to our breathing and continuing to sit quietly. This becomes much simpler as time goes on; and with practice, we eventually learn to rely on our breathing as a release valve for stress.

One method that can be used in meditation to alleviate stress is visualization. One of the beneficial aspects of such an activity is that it keeps the mind active and occupied. At the same time, visualization also provides a structure that enables the mind to de-stress and head in the direction of a more peaceful state of being. Instead of becoming bogged down in tension or attempting to run away from it, we will learn to maintain a steady position of awareness, allowing things to come and go with a greater sense of ease.

There are, of course, other options available for stress management, and many of these other tools, such as engaging in physical activity, can be of use to us in the present moment. However, when it comes to experiencing a long-term reduction in stress, the scientific evidence reveals that meditation is an effective intervention capable of transforming the physical morphology of the brain if we meditate consistently on a daily basis for a minimum of eight weeks (Ellwood, 2020). This is true, even with as little input as 10 minutes a day.

Cognitive Therapy for Stress

Our life can become more stressful if we dwell on negative thoughts. Being in a bad mood can negatively color our experience so that many of the things we experience seem more stressful and even overwhelming. It can also be contagious and can even cause others to treat us in a less friendly way, thus perpetuating negativity in both ourselves and virtually everyone else we come into contact with to some degree.

It has been demonstrated that cognitive therapy is an effective method for treating a wide variety of conditions, including anxiety disorders, depression, and even extreme stress. Cognitive therapy, or a combination of cognitive therapy and behavioral therapy, can be a very successful technique of treatment for stress, regardless of whether the stress is causing mood disorders or unpleasant sensations that are getting in the way of living a happy lifestyle.

The Theory That Supports Cognitive Therapy

The assumption upon which cognitive therapy for stress is based is that it is not merely the occurrences in our life that are the source of our stress, but rather the way in which we think about those occurrences. For instance, two individuals can get stuck in traffic at the same time.

One might look at this circumstance as a chance to relax by listening to music, getting lost in thinking, or both, and becoming calmer as a result. Another person can grow stressed out by concentrating on the lost time or the sensation of being stuck in the situation. There are a multitude of ways in which our negative ideas and the manner in which we talk to ourselves can color our experiences. These can either result in a stress response being triggered or a calm demeanor being displayed.

The vast majority of the thought patterns that have a detrimental influence on our experiences can be classified into a handful of typical cognitive distortions.

Cognitive therapists help their clients identify negative thought patterns that they have developed over time and work with them to change those habits. You can even complete some of them in the comfort of your own home.

Using Cognitive Therapy as a Means of Stress Relief

The findings of studies on optimistic and pessimistic explanation styles lend credence to the usefulness of this method. Cognitive therapy for stress, or a combination of cognitive and behavioral therapy, can also have beneficial results. Mindfulness meditation has also been used in cognitive treatment. This resulted in the development of a combination therapy called mindfulness-based cognitive therapy, which has also demonstrated some promising outcomes (Sipe & Eisendrath, 2012).

A great number of people have discovered that a cognitive approach is not only extraordinarily useful, but also far more expedient than other therapy approaches. This is a lot quicker than psychoanalytic therapy, which is what a lot of people still think of when they think of going to see an expert on stress relief.

How Does Cognitive Therapy Help With Stress?

In cognitive therapy, you should follow these steps:

- Find out why certain situations cause you to react in a stressful manner and how you can avoid them.
- Discover the ways in which you think and act that might be preventing you from feeling better, and learn how to change those patterns.
- Learn new ways of thinking and acting that can remove some of the stress elements in your life. By doing so, you can make it possible to cope better with events that cannot be avoided and have the potential to cause you to feel stressed.
- Acquire a fresh perspective and boost your self-assurance in your ability to deal with challenging situations in the days and years to come.

Putting It to the Test

You might try looking for someone who is an expert in cognitive therapeutic techniques. Ask potential therapists about their prior experience working with this method. You can start at home with some cognitive approaches to lower your stress levels if you are not interested in seeing a therapist at this time but would still like to try to lessen your levels of stress. You can learn to change your thinking habits with the assistance of a wide variety of resources, including online courses.

CHAPTER 8

Plasticity the Magic Power of the Mind

Plasticity is the amazing ability of the brain and mind to change, grow, and actively adapt to new conditions. This property is the source of many powers of your mind. The brain is able to change whenever a person goes through a new experience, regardless of whether or not it is a positive one.

Beliefs concerning the operation of the brain have undergone significant shifts over the course of time. In the past, scientists assumed that the brain was "fixed," but recent discoveries have proved that this assumption was incorrect and that the brain is actually more malleable. Up until the 1960s, researchers thought that changes in the brain could only take place in infants and children. It was thought that the physical anatomy of the brain was mostly set by the time a person reached early adulthood. After that, researchers discovered that brain plasticity is a continuous process throughout a person's lifetime.

What Is Plasticity?

As you read these lines, a change is taking place in your brain. The term "neuroplasticity" is used to describe this phenomenon. Your brain is constantly being reshaped, not just by the things you see, hear, touch, taste, and smell but also by the thoughts you think, which induce minute changes in its structure. In a sense, our ideas leave behind physical traces in the brain in much the same way that our footsteps leave behind impressions in the sand when we walk along the beach.

When you think, millions of neurons in your brain reach out and connect with each other, shaping the physical substance of your brain in the same way that a potter shapes clay. Neural connections are the connections that are made between different brain cells. One way to approach understanding neuroplasticity is to picture individual neurons as trees. Neurons have branches, and these branches reach out to link with the branches of other trees. New branches appear on the trees whenever there is an increase in activity in one particular region of the brain. Unnecessary branches will eventually die and fall off when activity levels decline.

Your Brain Adapts to the State of Your Mind

Many of us assume that the brain is an unchanging mass of organic matter that transmits encoded instructions to the rest of the body. However, the brain is not like this at all. It's a network of neurons and connections that's always shifting and adapting; and we're responsible for the shifts that are taking place.

Both our experiences and the thoughts that we believe cause changes in the brain. The changes that take place in your brain are not solely the result of your physical experiences, which are interpreted by your five senses.

Your ideas, thoughts, and beliefs, as well as the things you study,wish for, and dream about, all contribute to the formation of your brain.

The brain can be likened to a muscle that may be strengthened by using it. In the same way that muscular tissue grows when we engage in repeated bouts of exercise, certain parts of the brain also develop in thickness as we make use of them. This occurs when we repeatedly carry out the same action, envision the same thing, contemplate the same idea, experience the same emotion, or even dream the same dreams.

As an example, exam preparation can potentially cause physical changes to the brain. In fact, a study that was conducted in 2006 and published in the *Journal of Neuroscience* discovered changes in the brain maps of students who were studying for their examinations (Draganski et al., 2006). Brain imaging showed that the regions of the brain responsible for processing memory and abstract information were found to have thickened as a result of studying 38 medical students.

Let's imagine you have a history of being a complainer about various issues. You'll have built up brain maps that process your unpleasant thoughts and feelings. But let's say that you make the conscious decision to think more positively and shift your attention to the things for which you are grateful rather than irritate you. You now cultivate new maps that are capable of processing your revised style of thinking. Complaint-based maps start to shrink, while gratitude-based maps start to grow. Your new positive thankfulness map expands over time to become larger than the negative map that is based on complaints.

At the brain level, thinking positively and practicing thankfulness can eventually become habits. Your brain has been rewired to accommodate these new behaviors, and, as a result, you have become a completely different person.

A change of heart is all that is required for us to start the process of reshaping our brains. The brain reacts to the mental and emotional shifts that we experience; and over time, as it generates new maps, we will find that we do not require as much effort to accomplish the same tasks.

The new pattern of behavior has been ingrained and has developed into a habit.

Plasticity in Childhood

Even though plasticity can take place at any point in one's life, there are ages at which certain kinds of changes are more prevalent than others. For example, when the young brain grows and organizes itself throughout the first decade of life, there is a tendency for the brain to undergo significant changes during this time.

In general, young brains have a tendency to be more sensitive and responsive to the experiences they have than brains that are significantly older. However, this does not mean that the brains of adults are incapable of changing or adapting.

The brain of an infant and young child develops quickly throughout the first few years of life. When a person is born, every neuron in the cerebral cortex has approximately 2,500 synapses, which are the tiny gaps between neurons that allow nerve impulses to be transmitted. By the time a child reaches the age of three, this number has ballooned to a staggering 15,000 synapses per neuron. On the other hand, a typical adult has just around half of that amount of synapses in their 112 brain. Why? Because as we acquire new experiences, certain connections become stronger while others become weaker or disappear entirely. "Synaptic pruning" is the term used to describe this process.

The brain is able to adjust to new circumstances by forming new connections and discarding ineffective ones. Neurons that are activated more frequently form connections that are more robust. Those that are utilized infrequently or not at all eventually become obsolete.

Experience and Brain's Capacity for Change

Initial studies on the effect of experience on brain development suggested that significant alterations in one's environment would be required to have an effect on the maturation of the brain. However, we now understand that an unusually wide variety of experiences can change brain development and that some experiences can have a significant impact on how the brain develops despite appearing to be relatively harmless.

We will provide a summary of some of the effects that have received the most attention from researchers, with an emphasis on studies conducted on laboratory animals.

We will also cover the effects on functions that are exclusive to humans, such as language. We will not go over the repercussions of early brain injury because they will be covered in another section.

Three Types of Plasticity in Childhood

One distinctive characteristic of the developing brain is the capacity for three distinct types of plasticity: experience-independent, experience-expectant, and experiencedependent plasticity.

The notion that the genome provides a rough approximation of neural connectivity and that this connectivity can be modified by both internal and external events is the basis for experience-independent plasticity. Neurons that are active together strengthen their connections, but neurons that aren't active together at the same time are more likely to have weaker connections.

Most experience-expectant plasticity takes place in the early stages of development after birth. A child who is brought up hearing Korean, for instance, will be exposed to different speech sounds than a child who is brought up in an environment where English is spoken. During the first few months of life, infants are capable of differentiating the speech sounds of all languages.

However, as the infant's hearing system develops throughout the first year, it changes in such a way that the child becomes adept at differentiating the sounds in its native language context but loses the ability to differentiate foreign sounds.

The process of experience-dependent plasticity, in which the connections of groups of neurons are modified as a result of experience, begins soon after birth and continues throughout an individual's entire lifetime. One typical illustration of this can be observed in the results of what is known as "enriched experiences." Neuron parts called dendrites have the unique ability to rapidly change their shape in response to new information, potentially forming new synapses within a matter of minutes.

Critical Periods of Plasticity

The occurrence of critical periods is yet another one of the distinctive characteristics of plasticity, and it is particularly important for experience-expectant plasticity. One of the most well-studied models was initially reported by Wiesel and Hubel (Persons, 2023).

In this model, they demonstrated that if one eye of a kitten is kept closed after birth, the open eye will expand its territory at the expense of the eye that has been kept closed. When the eye that had been covered for a few months is eventually uncovered, the vision in that eye is impaired, which results in a permanent loss of the ability to see in space (amblyopia). The timing of the critical periods varies across the different regions of the brain because it is determined by the maturation of the inhibitory circuits. As molecular brakes reduce plasticity, the critical period comes to an end.

Stress and Brain Plasticity

Stress can cause changes in the way neurons in the hippocampus, amygdala, and prefrontal cortex of an adult's brain are structured. Studies have revealed that the density of neural connections decreases in the medial prefrontal cortex, but similar characteristics increase in the orbital frontal cortex as a result of stress. There are also changes in gene expression in the various parts of the brain, with each region revealing a different pattern of changed gene expression (Alexandra Kredlow et al., 2022).

Post-traumatic Stress Disorder and Stress

Any traumatic experience, whether you survived a war or the death of a loved one, has the potential to disrupt the normal neuronal connections in your brain, which can lead to Post-Traumatic Stress Disorder (PTSD). There is a possibility that you will have flashbacks, which will force you to relive the same traumatic event over and over again. Sometimes, your brain will exaggerate the scenario even further, which can lead to a somewhat skewed perception due to the fact that your subjective experience and heightened emotions are contributing factors. As a consequence of this, you might discover that you are unable to get enough sleep, are plagued by recurring nightmares, and struggle to function normally in social settings.

The fact of the matter is that the brain is adaptable and enjoys new experiences. According to one definition, neuroplasticity is the capacity of the brain to generate new neural connections in order to recover from an injury or disease. Sometimes, we are the ones who prevent our brains from changing because we are unable to get past a certain point. We are unable to wriggle our way out of this predicament or wake up from this never-ending nightmare. However, it is important to keep in mind that consistent positive experiences can also transform your brain, thanks to neuroplasticity.

Early Stress and Brain Plasticity

Stress at a young age puts individuals at a higher risk for a variety of maladaptive behaviors and psychopathologies, such as schizophrenia, depression, and addiction to drugs. Early stress also increases the risk of death from cardiovascular disease. An elevated and prolonged stress response, increased anxiety, impaired learning and memory, deficits in attention, altered exploratory behavior, altered social and play behavior, and an increased preference for alcohol are some of the behavioral abnormalities that can be caused by stress before and after birth in laboratory rodents (Haq et al., 2021).

There is a growing body of evidence suggesting that even preconception stress in either parent may have an effect on the offspring by causing changes in the adult offspring's behavior and brain appearance (Haq et al., 2021). The children in studies on the consequences of preconception paternal stress showed higher anxiety and impairment in a skillful reaching task. In addition, there were anomalies in neural connections that fluctuated dramatically throughout development.

Studies on the consequences of fetal stress have indicated, in general, that the offspring display higher anxiety, changed play behavior, and impaired behavioral and cognitive development (Glover, 2019). They demonstrate reductions in overall brain weight but not overall body weight. They also reveal reductions in neural connection density in some parts of the brain but increases in other parts, both of which are linked with changes in gene expression in these regions. Even though the physical pattern is distinct, the behavioral changes brought on by both preconception stress and fetal stress are very similar.

A study on the consequences of the ice storm that occurred in Quebec, Canada in 1998 is being used to investigate the effects that stress during pregnancy has on humans. The storm struck in the middle of winter, and it is estimated that about 2 million people were without electricity for up to six weeks during the month that is traditionally the coldest of the year. A large number of pregnant women were experiencing varying degrees of difficulty at various times of their pregnancies. Research has been conducted on the children of these women ranging from 2 to over 10 years of age. The children of stressed moms show abnormalities in cognitive, language development, and motor development, as well as play (CBC News, 2014).

The development of the brain can also be altered by stress after birth. A change in the hypothalamic-pituitary-adrenal axis occurs when there is a brief separation from the mother. This makes the axis more effective and facilitates faster recovery from the effects of stress.

However, there is a threshold beyond which the benefits of maternal separation become counterproductive.

Longer times (for example, three hours every day) led to greater anxiety in adult male offspring, disordered play behavior in both sexes, lower brain weight, and increased neural connections in specific regions of the brain (Renard et al., 2007). Therefore, it would appear that brief intervals of maternal separation are helpful to later adult conduct, but extended periods of maternal separation appear to have the reverse impact.

In conclusion, stress before conception, during pregnancy, and after birth all alter behavior and brain appearance, albeit in unique ways and rather dissimilarly from one another and from stress experienced during other stages of life.

Brain Plasticity After Physical Trauma

Researchers in the modern era have also discovered evidence that the brain is able to rewire itself after it has been injured. In the 1960s, researchers started investigating cases in which elderly persons who had suffered large strokes were able to restore functioning.

These cases demonstrated that the brain was more pliable than was previously supposed.

Researchers are now able to examine the inner workings of the brain in a way that was never previously feasible, thanks to advancements in technology. Research has shown that humans are not restricted to the mental capacities they are born with and that injured brains are often quite capable of extraordinary transformation (Puderbaugh & Emmady, 2021). This is one of the many discoveries as the study of modern neuroscience has flourished.

After damage to the brain, such as one caused by an accident or a stroke, the portions of the brain that were not harmed might re-organize themselves and take up the functions that were previously performed by the injured parts. This process moves at a variable pace, but it may move quickly for the first few weeks during the phase of spontaneous recovery, after which it may move more slowly. Rehabilitative programs, which can range from speech therapy to retraining certain types of movement, can be of assistance in this regard, and the nature of these programs depends on the severity of the damage.

Rehabilitation methods that are founded on the concept of a malleable brain have proven to be beneficial for millions of individuals. The present body of knowledge on neuroplasticity is already affecting therapeutic practices and is a vital topic to comprehend for anyone interested in the field of brain rehabilitation, despite the fact that research is still being conducted in this fascinating field at this time (Puderbaugh & Emmady, 2021).

Walking, chatting, and writing are all examples of activities that are performed repeatedly throughout the day. Because the actions are so deeply embedded in our consciousness, we no longer need to make an effort to carry them out; rather, we perform them automatically.

The efficiency of these electrical messaging processes can be attributed to the fact that they have followed the same path a large number of times.

If damage is sustained along a neural pathway, the brain will attempt to reorganize itself in order to re-route information down a neural pathway that has not been harmed. This does not occur in a single instant. Creating a new neural pathway requires a significant amount of work in the form of practice and repetition. Messages can take longer to arrive at their destination because even when a new pathway is constructed, it is not as efficient as the original. This explains why persons with brain damage become slower at motions, speaking, and thinking, as well as why they commonly report feeling weary.

Principles of Neural Rehabilitation

1. **Engagement:** The degree to which a person participates in the rehabilitation process can have a substantial impact on the outcome of the procedure.

Nothing is more frustrating than wasting hours of your life on activities that you have no interest in pursuing. The efficacy of the rehabilitation and, hence, the likelihood of its being successful can be partially determined by the degree of emotional engagement and attachment felt by the participant during the recovery sessions. When an individual places a higher priority on their rehabilitation, they are more likely to retain the abilities that they acquire during the treatment process.

2. **Intensity:** When we talk about the intensity of training, we are referring to how strenuous or involved recovery training is. It is necessary to reach a particular level of training intensity in order for neuroplasticity to take place.

3. **Repetition:** Your brain's neuroplasticity gives it the ability to rewire itself in response to repeated experiences, allowing it to devote more brain cells to a particular endeavor. Repetition is the most effective method–and possibly the only one that can be relied upon–for promoting this. Because your brain excels at the activities it engages in most frequently, it is essential to practice whatever it is you want to become proficient at.

4. **Duration:** Structural and functional changes take time. The amount of time that is spent carrying out the activity is a significant factor because the outcomes do not occur immediately. The question "How much time until I get better?" is the million-dollar question, but the answer generally varies from person to person and injury to injury.

How to Improve Your Brain's Plasticity

At any age, you may take actions that will help encourage your brain to adapt and change. The following is a set of measures to help you along this path:

Enrich Your Environment

It has been demonstrated that the brain undergoes favorable changes when a student is exposed to a learning environment that provides an abundance of possibilities for focused attention, novelty, and challenge. This is of utmost significance during the years of childhood and adolescence, but the benefits of a stimulating environment can be experienced far into adulthood if one chooses to do so. Stimulating your brain can mean any of the following (Baroncelli et al., 2009):

- Traveling and discovering new locations
- Reading
- Learning a new language
- Obtaining the skills to perform an instrument
- Making art and engaging in other creative endeavors

Get a Good Deal of Sleep

It has been established that sleep plays a significant role in the maintenance of both physical and mental health.

The process of forming new neural connections in the brain has been proven to be significantly affected by sleep. It's possible that you can induce greater brain plasticity by expanding and fortifying these connections.

By maintaining healthy sleeping habits, you can enhance the quality of your sleep. Among these are the establishment of a reliable pattern for one's sleeping habits as well as the provision of a setting that promotes restful sleep.

Exercise Regularly

According to a study that was published in 2021, regular physical activity appears to increase brain plasticity in a number of different ways (Umegaki et al., 2021). These include its effect on the brain-derived neurotrophic factor (BDNF), which is a protein that influences neuron growth; functional connectivity; and the basal ganglia, which is the region of the brain that is responsible for learning and motor control.

Participating in regular physical activity has a variety of positive effects on the brain. Exercising could potentially help prevent the death of neurons in critical regions of the hippocampus, which is a component of the brain that is responsible for remembering as well as other tasks (Liu & Nusslock, 2018). The findings of studies suggest that this region of the brain may be involved in the production of new neurons in response to physical activity.

The United States Department of Health and Human Services suggests getting at least 150 minutes of moderate-intensity cardio exercises (such as walking, dancing, swimming, or cycling) per week and a minimum of two days of strength training exercises (lifting weights or doing bodyweight exercises) (CDC, 2019).

Children aren't the only ones who can enjoy playing games: The neuroplasticity of your brain can be improved by playing games like board games, card games, video games, and even other types of games.

Try Your Hand at Some Meditation

Learning that meditation also alters the brain might not come as much of a surprise to some people. A number of studies have shown that meditation can promote neuroplasticity. For example, a study of meditation practitioners who used the Buddhist "Insight" meditation at Massachusetts General Hospital showed that the thickness of the prefrontal cortex of the brain had increased (Lazar et al., 2005). The prefrontal cortex is the region that controls concentration; therefore, this finding is significant.

Practice Attention and Mindfulness

One of the most straightforward approaches to meditation is known as mindfulness, and one of the most straightforward methods for practicing mindfulness is to simply bring your attention to the fact that you are breathing. When we focus our attention on our breathing, we engage the prefrontal cortex of the brain, which in turn causes it to develop in a manner analogous to a muscle. The prefrontal cortex is like the CEO of the brain because it is responsible for controlling things like attention, compassion, free will, and even the capacity to control ourselves and override instinctive emotional responses. Because of this, the practice of mindfulness has been linked to gains in each of these domains.

A key component of practicing mindfulness is bringing one's full attention to the hereand-now without allowing one's thoughts to wander to either the past or future. The ability to be conscious of the sights, sounds, and sensations that are occurring around you is essential. As you can see, numerous studies have demonstrated that the cultivation of attention and regular practice of mindfulness can encourage neuroplasticity in the brain.

CONCLUSION

Your mind has a lot more power over your body than you give it credit for. You have the ability to comprehend the mind-body link and put it to good use in order to enhance both your mental and physical health as well as your overall well-being. Even though scientists have known for a long time that our emotions and thoughts can have an effect on our bodies, we are just starting to understand how these connections work.

Altering the way you think and taking responsibility for the thoughts that run through your head can have a positive impact on your overall physical health. Even if having a positive attitude won't fix everything, having a healthy mindset is an essential part of maintaining a healthy physique.

This book is an engaging introduction to the body-mind connection for all interested in the subject. It emphasizes the scientific evidence for the importance of the body-mind relationship. It reviews the scientific evidence that mental ideas can impact and control biological processes, and offers practical advice on utilizing this phenomenon to the best advantage.

I hope that this book will encourage you to unleash the amazing power of your mind to improve your physical and mental well-being. It is my sincere wish that those who are in need of encouragement and sound advice will find both in this book.

References

Alexandra Kredlow, M., Fenster, R. J., Laurent, E. S., Ressler, K. J., & Phelps, E. A. (2022). Prefrontal cortex, amygdala, and threat processing: Implications for PTSD. Neuropsychopharmacology, *47*(1), 247–259. https://doi.org/10.1038/ s41386-021-01155-7

Baroncelli, L., Braschi, C., Spolidoro, M., Begenisic, T., Sale, A., & Maffei, L. (2009). Nurturing brain plasticity: Impact of environmental enrichment. Cell Death & Differentiation, 17*(7), 1092–1103*. https://doi.org/10.1038/cdd.2009.193

Benedetti, F., & Piedimonte, A. (2019). The neurobiological underpinnings of placebo and nocebo effects. *Seminars in Arthritis and Rheumatism, 49(* 3), S18–S21. https://doi.org/10.1016/j.semarthrit.2019.09.015

Branthwaite, A., & Cooper, P. (1981). Analgesic effects of branding in treatment of headaches. *BMJ,* 133 *282*(6276), 1576-1578. https://doi.org/10.1136/bmj.282.6276.1576

Bräscher, A.-K., Witthöft, M., & Becker, S. (2018). The underestimated significance of conditioning in placebo hypoalgesia and nocebo hyperalgesia. Pain Research and Management, 2018*, 1–8*. https://doi.org/10.1155/2018/6841985

Cascio, C. N., O'Donnell, M. B., Tinney, F. J., Lieberman, M. D., Taylor, S. E., Strecher, V. J., & Falk, E. B. (2015). Self-affirmation activates brain systems associated with self-related processing and reward and is reinforced by future orientation.

Social Cognitive and Affective Neuroscience, 11*(4), 621–629. https:/ / doi.org/*10.1093/scan/nsv136 Case, L. K., Jackson, P., Kinkel, R., & Mills, P. J. (2018).

Guided imagery improves mood, fatigue, and quality of life in individuals with multiple sclerosis: An exploratory efficacy trial of healing light guided imagery. *Journal of Evidence Based Integrative Medicine, 23,* 2515690X1774874. https://doi.org/10.1177/2515690x17748744

CBC News. (2014). Ice storm stress affected pregnant women's offspring, study suggests. *CBC.* https://www.cbc.ca/news/canada/montreal/ice-storm-stressaffected-pregnant-women-s-offspring-study-suggests-1.2781661

CDC. (2019). How much physical activity do older adults need? CDC. https://www.cdc.gov/physicalactivity/basics/older_adult s/index.htm

Charalambous, A., Giannakopoulou, M., Bozas, E., Marcou, Y., Kitsios, P., & Paikousis, L. (2016). Guided imagery and progressive muscle relaxation as a cluster of symptoms management intervention in patients receiving chemotherapy: A randomized control trial. *PLoS One, 11*(6), e0156911. https://doi.org/10.1371/journal.pone.0156911

Cohen, S., Alper, C. M., Doyle, W. J., Treanor, J. J., & Turner, R. B. (2006). Positive emotional style predicts resistance to illness after experimental exposure to rhinovirus or influenza A virus. Psychosomatic Medicine, *68*(6), 809–815. https://doi.org/10.1097/01.psy.0000245867.92364.3c

Critcher, C. R., & Dunning, D. (2014). Self-Affirmations provide a broader perspective on self-threat. Personality and Social Psychology Bulletin, 41*(1), 3–18. https://*doi.org/10.1177/0146167214554956

de Craen, A. J. M., Tijssen, J. G. P., de Gans, J., & Kleijnen, J. (2000). Placebo effect in the acute treatment of migraine: Subcutaneous placebos are better than oral placebos. *Journal of Neurology, 247(* 3), 183–188. https://doi.org/10.1007/ s004150050560

Donaldson, V. W. (2000). A clinical study of visualization on depressed white blood cell count in medical patients. Applied

Psychophysiology and Biofeedback, *25*(2), 117–128. https://doi.org/10.1023/a:1009518925859

Draganski, B., Gaser, C., Kempermann, G., Kuhn, H. G., Winkler, J., Buchel, C., & May, A. (2006). Temporal and spatial dynamics of brain structure changes during extensive learning. *Journal of Neuroscience, 26*(23), 6314–6317. https://doi.org/10.1523/jneurosci.4628-05.2006

Duke Health News. (2003). Positive outlook linked to longer life in heart patients. *Duke Health.* https://corporate.dukehealth.org/news/positive-outlook-linked-longerlife-heart-patients

Ellwood, B. (2020, March 22). Daily meditation decreases anxiety and improves cognitive functioning in new meditators after 8 weeks. PsyPost. https://www.psypost.org/2020/03/daily-meditation-decreases-anxiety-and improvesc ognitive-functioning-in-new-meditators-after-8- weeks-56198#:~:text=Only%208%20weeks%20of%20daily

Eremin, O., Walker, M. B., Simpson, E., Heys, S. D., Ah-See, A. K., Hutcheon, A. W., Ogston, K. N., Sarkar, T. K., Segar, A., & Walker, L. G. (2009). Immunomodulatory effects of relaxation training and guided imagery in women with locally advanced breast cancer undergoing multimodality therapy: A randomised controlled trial. *The Breast, 18*(1), 17–25. https://doi.org/10.1016/j.breast.2008.09.002

Giltay, E. J., Geleijnse, J. M., Zitman, F. G., Hoekstra, T., & Schouten, E. G. (2004). Dispositional optimism and all-cause and cardiovascular mortality in a prospective cohort of elderly Dutch men and women. *Archives of General Psychiatry, 61*(11), 1126. https://doi.org/10.1001/archpsyc.61.11.1126

Glover, V. (2019). Stress and pregnancy (prenatal and perinatal) | the effects of prenatal stress on child behavioural and cognitive outcomes start at the beginning. *Encyclopedia on Early Childhood Development.*

https://www.childencyclopedia.com/stress-and-pregnancy-prenatal-and-perinatal/accordingexperts/effects-prenatal-stress-child

Haour, F. (2005). Mechanisms of the placebo effect and of conditioning. *Neuroimmunomodulation, 12*(4), 195–200. https://doi.org/10.1159/000085651

Haq, S. U., Bhat, U. A., & Kumar, A. (2021). Prenatal stress effects on offspring brain and behavior: Mediators, alterations and dysregulated epigenetic mechanisms. *Journal of Biosciences, 46, 34.* https://pubmed.ncbi.nlm.nih.gov/33859069/

Kivimäki, M., & Kawachi, I. (2015). Work stress as a risk factor for cardiovascular disease. *Current Cardiology* Reports, 17(9*).* https://doi.org/10.1007/ s11886-015-0630-8

Kirchhof, J., Petrakova, L., Brinkhoff, A., Benson, S., Schmidt, J., Unteroberdörster, M., Wilde, B., Kaptchuk, T. J., Witzke, O., & Schedlowski, M. (2018). Learned immunosuppressive placebo responses in renal transplant patients. Proceedings of the National Academy of Sciences *139* of the United States of America, 115*(16), 4223–*4227. https://doi.org/10.1073/pnas.1720548115

Kong, J., Kaptchuk, T. J., Polich, G., Kirsch, I., & Gollub, R. L. (2007). Placebo analgesia: Findings from brain imaging studies and emerging hypotheses. Reviews in the Neurosciences, *18*(3-4). https://doi.org/10.1515/revneuro.2007.18.3-4.173

Lazar, S. W., Kerr, C. E., Wasserman, R. H., Gray, J. R., Greve, D. N., Treadway, M. T., McGarvey, M., Quinn, B. T., Dusek, J. A., Benson, H., Rauch, S. L., Moore, C. I., & Fischl, B. (2005). Meditation experience is associated with increased cortical thickness. *Neuroreport, 16*(17), 1893–1897.

https://doi.org/10.1097/01.wnr.0000186598.66243.19

Levine, J. (1978). The mechanisms of placebo analgesia. The Lancet, *312*(8091), 654–657. https://doi.org/10.1016/s0140-

6736(78)92762-9

Lindquist, R., Snyder, M., & Mary Frances Tracy. (2013). Complementary & alternative therapies in *nursing seventh edition.* New York Springer Publishing Company Ann Arbor, Michigan Proquest. Liu, P. Z., & Nusslock, R. (2018). Exercise-Mediated neurogenesis in the hippocampus via BDNF. Frontiers in Neuroscience, *12*(52). https://doi.org/10.3389/ fnins.2018.00052

Liu, Y., Hou, Y., Quan, H., Zhao, D., Zhao, J., Cao, B., Pang, Y., Chen, H., Lei, X., & Yuan, H. (2023). Mindfulness training improves attention: Evidence from behavioral and event-related potential analyses. *Brain Topography, 36(2*). https://doi.org/10.1007/ s10548-023-00938-z

Luders, E., Kurth, F., Mayer, E. A., Toga, A. W., Narr, K. L., & Gaser, C. (2012). The unique brain anatomy of meditation practitioners: Alterations in cortical gyrification . *Frontiers in Human Neuroscience, 6*. https://doi.org/10.3389/ fnhum.2012.00034

Merschel, M. (2022). The promise of meditation for the heart and mind. *Heart. https://*www.heart.org/en/news/2022/06/16/the-promise-of-meditation-for-the-heartand-mind

Mrazek, M. D., Franklin, M. S., Phillips, D. T., Baird, B., & Schooler, J. W. (2013). Mindfulness Training Improves Working Memory Capacity and GRE Performance While Reducing Mind Wandering. Psychological Science, *24*(5), 776–781. https://doi.org/10.1177/0956797612459659

Nguyen, J., & Brymer, E. (2018). Nature-Based guided imagery as an intervention for state anxiety. Frontiers in Psychology, *9*. https://doi.org/10.3389/ fpsyg.2018.01858

Park, S. Q., Kahnt, T., Dogan, A., Strang, S., Fehr, E., & Tobler, P. N. (2017). A neural link between generosity and happiness. Nature Communications, *8*(15964), 15964. https://doi.org/10.1038/ ncomms15964

Patel, J. (2019). Consequences of repression of emotion: Physical health, mental health and general well being. *International Journal of Psychotherapy Practice* and Research, *1*(3), 16–21. https://doi.org/10.14302/issn.2574-612X.ijpr-18-2564

Persons, M. (2023). *A nobel partnership: Hubel & Wiesel.* Harvard University Brain Tour. https://braintour.harvard.edu/archives/portfolio-items/hubel-and-wiesel Puderbaugh, M., & Emmady, P. D. (2021). *Neuroplasticity.* StatPearls Publishing. https://pubmed.ncbi.nlm.nih.gov/32491743/

Renard, G. M., Rivarola, M. A., & Suárez, M. M. (2007). Sexual dimorphism in rats: Effects of early maternal separation and variable chronic stress on pituitaryadrenal axis and behavior. *International Journal of Developmental Neuroscience, 25*(6), 373–379.

https://doi.org/10.1016/j.ijdevneu.2007.07.001

Robertson, D. (2009, June 17). *Émile coué's method of* "conscious autosuggestion." *UK* College of Hypnosis & Hypnotherapy. https://www.ukhypnosis.com/2009/06/17/emile-coues-method-of-conscious-autosuggestion/

Roffe, L., Schmidt, K., & Ernst, E. (2005). A systematic review of guided imagery as an adjuvant cancer therapy. *Psycho-Oncology, 14*(8), 607–617. https://doi.org/10.1002/pon.889

Segerstrom, S. C., & Miller, G. E. (2004). Psychological stress and the human immune system: A meta-analytic study of 30 years of inquiry. *Psychological Bulletin, 130*(4), 601–630. https://doi.org/10.1037/0033-2909.130.4.601

Sipe, W. E. B., & Eisendrath, S. J. (2012). Mindfulness-Based cognitivetherapy:Theoryandpractice. *TheCanadianJournalof Psychiatry, 57*(2), 63–69. https:// doi.org/10.1177/070674371205700202

Smith, T. W., Uchino, B. N., Berg, C. A., Florsheim, P., Pearce, G., Hawkins, M., Hopkins, P. N., & Yoon, H.-C. (2007). Hostile personality traits and coronary artery calcification in middle-aged and older married couples: Different effects for self-144 reports versus spouse ratings. *Psychosomatic Medicine, 69*(5), 441–448. https://doi.org/10.1097/psy.0b013e3180600a65

Steele, C. M. (1988, January 1). The psychology of self-affirmation: Sustaining the integrity of the self. Science Direct. https://www.sciencedirect.com/science/article/abs/pii/S0065260108602294

Umegaki, H., Sakurai, T., & Arai, H. (2021). Active life for brain health: A narrative review of the mechanism underlying the protective effects of physical activity on the brain. *Frontiers in Aging Neuroscience,* 13. https://doi.org/10.3389/fnagi.2021.761674